AF808875

EASY MONEY MANAGEMENT WEEKLY JOURNAL

52 MEDITATIONS TO REVOLUTIONIZE HOW YOU THINK ABOUT MONEY

BY

Laurick Ingram

Be sure to go to my website
giveandsave365.com
for bonus materials like my free
ONE-YEAR / ONE-PAGE PERSONAL MONEY MANAGEMENT PLAN.

EASY MONEY MANAGEMENT WEEKLY JOURNAL
© 2018 Laurick Ingram
All rights reserved
ISBN: 978-0-9991716-4-6

No part of this book may be reproduced or transmitted in any form or by any means, graphic, electronic, or mechanical, including photocopying, recording, taping, or by any information storage retrieval system, without permission, in writing, of the author.

"Poverty is attracted to the mind of the one who is favorable to it, as money is attracted to one whose mind has been deliberately prepared to attract it, and through the same laws."

—Napoleon Hill *Think and Grow Rich*

"The core concept of The Give and Save 3-6-5 Project is to create prosperity through philanthropy. It is founded in the belief that you can grow your giving by faith and grow your faith by saving."

—Laurick Ingram, Director
Give and Save 365, LLC

PREFACE

In matters of money, during my life I have met two types of people. Those who constantly need more money than they have and those who consistently have more money than they need. The good news is that if you or someone you know is in the first group, you or that person can change: I did. The differences in these two types are what they think and believe about money. Those thoughts and beliefs are the spirit that governs what they do with their money and what their money does for them. That spirit either attracts money to them or repels money from them. This book is designed to empower your spirit to attract money to you.

Three questions will let you know if this book is of value to you:

(1) Do you believe that next week you will have more money than you have this week?

(2) Do you believe next week that you will have done better for yourself and others with the money you have?

(3) Do you believe that next week you will know more about what to do with your money and what your money can do for you?

If you answered "yes" to all three, this book will probably only reinforce what you already think and believe. If you answered, "I don't know, maybe, or no" to any of the questions, then this book can get you to "YES!"

This book contains one idea a week for you to think and act on until it becomes such a strong belief that doing it becomes automatic and necessary, like brushing your teeth when you wake up in the morning. We, at Give and Save 3-6-5, know that thinking good thoughts about money is something you should do 365 days a year, because for every day you do not do it, someone else will be helping you to think of ways to send your money to them.

Read the following meditations at the beginning of your week. Then repeat them and look for ways to prove and use them in your own life. Write them down, or text or e-mail them to yourself and a friend. Discuss them and share your thoughts with us on our website, https://giveandsave365.com/ or on social media. Do this and we guarantee before the year is done, your positive beliefs about money will cause you to see new opportunities for money to come pouring into your lives. There is a line from the movie, *The Shawshank Redemption* that goes, "Get busy living, or get busy dying." When it comes to your money, I say get busy getting, giving, and saving it, or get busy losing, scrimping, and wasting it. It is up to you, but if you want to get busy getting, giving, and saving it, the getting starts with your mind-set, and these ideas will help you create and maintain a winning money mind-set.

Let's get started!

(Note: If you bought this book as an E-book, you can go to the "RESOURCES" tab on my website and download the worksheet that follows each meditation.)

Week 1

"A journey of a thousand miles begins with a single step."
—Lao Tzu, Chinese philosopher

My Thought for the Week

My 365-day journey toward developing a lifetime habit of giving and saving begins today. Every day, I will remind myself that whenever I get money, I will give some away and save some for myself. When the money comes—and it will—I will donate some to a person, group, organization, or cause; and for every dollar I give away, I will save one for myself.

My Action Step

I will keep my first saved dollar in a secure place and give my first gift dollar to my church.

Date:

Your thought for the week: Where will you keep your first dollar to remind you of the day you decided to give and save?

Your action step:

Week 2

"Whether you think you can, or you can't; either way, you're right."

—Henry Ford

My Thought for the Week

I was not good at packing my suitcase for trips, which I reminded myself of regularly and proved each time I took a trip. Once while on a trip in Chicago, I decided to go on the internet and watch some how-to videos on packing a suitcase. Rather than continue thinking I sucked at packing, I changed my thinking to *I can learn how to pack.* Within thirty minutes, the items in my suitcase were neatly and efficiently organized. When I thought I couldn't pack my suitcase neatly, I could not; when I thought I could, I did. I was right both times.

My Action Step

One of my brothers, who was working three jobs at the time, used to say repeatedly, "I can make money, but I can't manage money." He was right and repeatedly proved it in his financial decisions. For example, he had three jobs and bad credit. Even before I knew the Henry Ford quotation listed above, I began telling myself, "I can make and manage money." My brother thought he *couldn't* do something and was right. I thought I *could*, and I was right.

Date:

Your thought for the week: What things do you think you can or can't do with your money?

Your action step:

Week 3

"Now faith is the substance of things hoped for, the evidence of things not seen."

—The Bible

My Thought for the Week

It takes the same amount of energy to have faith that I will get what I am willing to focus on, hope for, and work for as it does to focus on what I don't have right now. I can choose to think about the things I want and how to get them rather than to believe that I never will have the things I do not have. If I want something I do not currently have, what I can currently have is the faith that I can get it.

My Action Step

The times in my life that I had no money and no job, I soldiered on, having faith that if I kept asking, kept seeking, and kept knocking, I would find both or they would find me. It worked.

Date:

Your thought for the week: What are you doing to demonstrate faith that the money you are seeking will come to you?

Your action step:

Week 4

"And when you want something, all the universe conspires in helping you to achieve it."

—Paulo Coelho, *The Alchemist*

My Thought for the Week

No matter how much I want something, I acknowledge there is a power greater than I am at work in the universe. My job is to broadcast my wants and then work and wait as my higher power transmits how those things will come to me.

My Action Step

If you want to travel somewhere, fix the location in your mind and then start planning even before you know how you will pay for it. You will be amazed first at how many people you will meet who will say they have been there. Next, you will begin to see offers of how to travel there. The more you want it, the more opportunities will be given to you to get it, but you must want it and believe the universe will help you get it.

Date:

Your thought for the week: Over the next year, how much money do you want to get, give, and save?

Your action step:

Week 5

"Arkad [a merchant and the richest man in Babylon] teaches the seven lessons for managing money. Lesson 1: for each ten coins I put in, to spend but nine."

—George Clason, *The Richest Man in Babylon*

My Thought for the Week

This is a cornerstone of strong money management, because it cuts two ways. First, it builds the habit of saving. Second, by spending less than you get, you continually remind yourself that you have more than you need.

My Action Step

I explained this to my grandniece this way: "Sweetie, if you spend every dollar you make as fast as you make it, at the end of the month, you still will not have everything you want because as humans, we can always find more to want. Plus, you will be broke. If you train yourself to save some of the money you get, at the end of the month, you still won't have everything you want, but at least, you will have more money saved than you did the month before."

Date:

Your thought for the week: Have you began giving and saving already? If not, then why not start today?

Your action step:

Week 6

"Lesson 2: Budget your expenses to pay for your necessities and pleasures without spending more than the nine coins you have left. (My plan includes giving one of the nine coins away and living off the remaining eight.)"

—George Clason, *The Richest Man in Babylon*

My Thought for the Week

It makes sense that I should not build a house without first counting the costs. Once I know how much I must spend, then I know that is what I should spend. If not, it will lead either to borrowing money, which now eats away at the money I have saved or chips away at my savings until there is nothing left.

My Action Step

In the late nineties, after much urging from my wife and much resistance from me, I began to bank online with much trepidation. In my mind, I imagined all the things that could go wrong by accessing my accounts online. None of those fears were ever realized. Online banking organized our records, tracked our expenses, saved on postage, and streamlined our bill paying. When it comes to budgeting, unless you are a math wizard who enjoys scribbling and figuring, either hire a bookkeeper or use your computer, tablet, or phone to do the heavy lifting in budgeting your money. I will not recommend a program or app, but there are many good ones out there.

Date:

Your thought for the week: What simple way do you have to keep track of what you are spending on what?

Your action step:

Week 7

"Lesson 3: Put your money to work creating an income for you."

—George Clason, *The Richest Man in Babylon*

My Thought for the Week

I understand that money is a tool, an item than can be exchanged for other things. Some things I buy will cost me money to maintain. This is not a bad thing. I pay to maintain the car that takes me back and forth to work. I pay for the electricity that powers my home. Some things I invest in, however, pay me money to own them. The stocks I own, the businesses I own, the real estate that generates rental income. One of the investments that cost me the least but pays me the most is my vocabulary—the money words I know—so I make sure I continually invest in my financial education.

My Action Step

I continually add to the money words I know and use them to make good decisions. I learn them through reading, writing, attending classes, online learning, conversing with others, and applying them to managing my money. Some of the words I know, and use are: *common stocks*, *mutual funds*, *exchange traded funds*, *return on investment*, *rate of return*, *price earnings ratio*, *S&P 500* (The Standard and Poor's 500 Index), *getting*, *giving*, and *saving money*.

Date:

Your thought for the week: List one way you are putting your money to work creating income for you.

Your action step:

Week 8

"Lesson 4: Guard your money from loss."

—George Clason, *The Richest Man in Babylon*

My Thought for the Week

Whenever I am considering financial opportunities, I remember to focus first on the return of my money and then on the return on my money. Some of the biggest scams have lured people in, because the people focused on the return *on* their money before ensuring the return *of* their money. People who have lost money to a Ponzi scheme are painfully aware of this. The returns initially seem incredible; however, your initial investment is not secure because it is used to pay and lure others into the scheme.

My Action Step

A reputable professional once asked me to invest in a limited partnership with him and some others to buy and sell real estate. When I did my cross-check, I learned the subcontractor had open cases with the Securities and Exchange Commission for mishandling investors' moneys in previous deals. Even though the professional suggested the return *on* my money would be 20 percent to 40 percent annually, the subcontractor's past deeds made the return *of* my money uncertain. I passed on the deal.

Date:

Your thought for the week: How are you making sure your money is safe?

Your action step:

Week 9

"Lesson 5: Own your own home."
—George Clason, *The Richest Man in Babylon*

My Thought for the Week

I have heard the notion that your home is not an asset. If the definition of an asset is something that generates income, a home does not fit that definition. However, I must have somewhere to lay my head, and I will either rent it or own it. I choose to own it.

My Action Step

I know an architect who chooses to rent a house on the beach rather than own it. In his case, it makes sense because he owns a lot of commercial real estate that pays in a good income. The only compelling argument I have heard for not owning a home is to use the money you would have invested in a home to invest elsewhere. Most of the people I have met who do not own homes also do not invest the money elsewhere. By owning a home, at least, they can accumulate value in real estate.

Date:

Your thought for the week: Do you either own your home or have a plan to own your home?

Your action step:

Week 10

"Lesson 6: Ensure a future income."
—George Clason, *The Richest Man in Babylon*

My Thought for the Week

My brother, Bobby (the late Reverend Robert Ingram, PhD), was seventy-one and getting dressed to go to one of his three jobs on the day he died. I knew my brother, and that is how he wanted it. Retirement was a dirty word. Nevertheless, from the time he was in his fifties, he had a retirement plan that paid him every month, and after he passed, it continued to pay his widow. He was favored with a razor-sharp mind and health that allowed him to continue working, but had he not been able to continue, he had guaranteed himself a future income.

My Action Step

I have insurance policies, real estate, and other assets that generate income for me now and in the future. Like my brother, I still work running my businesses, but a lot of my income comes from my money working for me.

Date:

Your thought for the week: What are you doing to ensure a future income for yourself?

Your action step:

Week 11

"Lesson 7: Study and become wiser, to become more skillful in handling your money."

—George Clason, *The Richest Man in Babylon*

My Thought for the Week

When performing tasks, risk is a function of competence. A fifteen-year-old who got his license yesterday is more likely to have a preventable accident than a twenty-five-year-old with ten-year safe-driving record. At this stage in my life, I can handle far more money with far less risk than I could have twenty years ago because I continue to study to become wiser and more skillful in the handling of my money. It doesn't mean my money journey will be accident-free; it means that each day, I am better at avoiding accidents and better prepared for the ones I cannot avoid.

My Action Step

I have a six-step affirmation card that I carry with me and put up in my bathroom to read in the morning when I awake. Affirmations four and five are as follows: I am so happy that (4) I constantly *learn*, and *teach* the strategies I use through home study courses, seminars, webinars, meetups, books, and articles listened to, written, or read; and (5) I continually retool, update, and improve my strategies while giving freely, yet judiciously of the knowledge, assets, wealth, and time I acquire along the way.

Date:

Your thought for the week: Name one thing you will do to become wiser and more skillful in handling your money.

Your action step:

Week 12

"I must teach my mind to train my money to treat me right."

—Laurick Ingram, Director
Give and Save 365, LLC

My Thought for the Week

In my quest to be an excellent money manager, I remind myself daily that my money can work for me, but I must train it to do so. If I do not train my money to remain with me and continue working for me and attracting more money to me, it will flee from me and fly to others who trained their money better.

My Action Step

I will teach myself the steps taught in this book that will train my money to remain with me and continue working for me and attracting more money to me.

Date:

Your thought for the week: In what way are you teaching your mind to train your money to work for you?

Your action step:

Week 13

"If the people have the advancing mind, have the faith that they can become rich, and move forward with the fixed purpose to become rich, nothing can possibly keep them in poverty."

—Wallace B. Wattles, *The Science of Getting Rich*

My Thought for the Week

I have an advancing mind; I have the faith that I can get, give, and save money; and I move forward with the fixed purpose to get, give, and save money; therefore, new money continually flows into my life.

My Action Step

My wife and I own a rental property free and clear that has paid us money every month from the time we bought it.

Date:

Your thought for the week: When it comes to your money, how are you advancing your mind, how strong is your faith, and what have you fixed in your mind?

Your action step:

Week 14

"You can set and achieve your goals more effectively with the help of a simple acronym. Make all your goals SMART—*Specific*, Measurable, Accountable, Realistic and Relevant, Time Line."

—Michael Gelb, *How to Think Like Leonardo da Vinci*

My Thought for the Week

"Specific: Define exactly what you want to accomplish, in detail." I have *specific* money goals when it comes to getting, giving, and saving money.

My Action Step

In 1985, I got a new job. Before I got my first paycheck, I filled out the form to have one hundred dollars automatically deducted from my check and deposited in my credit union savings account. I continued doing that for my entire career.

Date:

Your thought for the week: What specific money goals do you have?

Your action step:

Week 15

"You can set and achieve your goals more effectively with the help of a simple acronym—make all your goals SMART—Specific, *Measurable*, Accountability, Realistic and Relevant, Time Line."

—Michael Gelb, *How to Think like Leonardo da Vinci*

My Thought for the Week

"Measurable: Decide how you will measure your progress and most important, how you will know that you have achieved your goal." I have *measurable* goals when it comes to getting, giving, and saving money.

My Action Step

My wife and I used to take a couples' trip with two other married couples. For the first couple of years, when the trip was drawing near, we would sit down and spend hours figuring out how much we would spend on the trip. After the third time, I suggested we put a set amount in an account twice a month, and when the trip came, we would know how much we had and could plan the trip within that budget. We used that plan and one great lesson my wife and I learned from it was: Going on a vacation that is "paid for" is way more relaxing than going on one you charged on your credit card and must pay for months or years after the vacation is over.

Date:

Your thought for the week: What measurable money goals do you have?

Your action step:

Week 16

"You can set and achieve your goals more effectively with the help of a simple acronym—make all your goals SMART—Specific, Measurable, *Accountability*, Realistic and Relevant, Time Line."

—Michael Gelb, *How to Think like Leonardo da Vinci*

My Thought for the Week

"Accountability: Make a full commitment to be personally responsible for achieving your goal." I am *accountable* when it comes to getting, giving, and saving money.

My Action Step

Because I grew up as a child on welfare, my medical treatment came through public health assistance. Once, I was sick and had to go to the emergency room. I had to wait fourteen hours before a doctor saw me. I knew my health was my responsibility and I would be accountable to myself. As soon as I got a job, I purchased good health insurance and have never gone a day in my adult life without medical insurance for me, my wife, or my children.

Date:

Your thought for the week: List one way you take full responsibility for the money you get, give, and save.

Your action step:

Week 17

"You can set and achieve your goals more effectively with the help of a simple acronym—make all your goals SMART—Specific, Measurable, Accountability, *Realistic and Relevant*, Time Line."

—Michael Gelb, *How to Think like Leonardo da Vinci*

My Thought for the Week

"Realistic and Relevant: Set goals that are ambitious but achievable." I have *realistic and relevant* goals for my money.

My Action Step

Rather than say I want or need more money, I have set a realistic and relevant amount I need and know the precise reason I need it. I want to replace my older hurricane panel shutters with accordion hurricane shutters (I live in Florida, the land of hurricanes). It is realistic because I got three price quotes and know what it will cost and how much money I need to pay for them this year. It is relevant because it affects the safety of my family and my quality of life.

Date:

Your thought for the week: What one realistic and relevant goal do you have for your money this year?

Your action step:

Week 18

"You can set and achieve your goals more effectively with the help of a simple acronym—make all your goals SMART—Specific, Measurable, Accountability, Realistic and Relevant, *Time Line*."

—Michael Gelb, *How to Think like Leonardo da Vinci*

My Thought for the Week

"Time Line: Create a Time Line for achieving your goals." I have a *time line* for achieving my goals, so I know when I expect to get, give, and save my money.

My Action Step

When our sons were born, my wife and I knew that eighteen years from that point, we would need money for their college educations. Eighteen years was our time line, and every two weeks, money went into two investment accounts for them. When they turned eighteen, the moneys were there.

Date:

Your thought for the week: What do you need money for, when do you need it, and what are you doing to make sure it will be there when you need it?

Your action step:

Week 19

"Confidence comes not from always being right, but from not fearing to be wrong."

—Peter T. McIntire

My Thought for the Week

I understand there will be times I am wrong in matters of money. When I am wrong, I will accept it quickly, learn as much as I can from it, and then go forward with more knowledge and experience than I had before the mistake.

My Action Step

My first semester in college, I got four As and an F. I got the F because, once I decided to drop the class, I stopped going, but I let the deadline for dropping the class pass. Try though I might, I have never been able to get that F off my transcripts, but after that, I never missed another deadline in college. To make it worse, I still had to pay for the class, or the college would not release my grades. Since then, I have never missed a deadline in college and I always paid all my college expenses, including my student loan.

Date:

Your thought for the week: What one money decision were you wrong about, and what did you learn from it?

Your action step:

Week 20

"No one who can rise before dawn 360 days a year fails to make his family rich."

—Chinese Proverb

My Thought for the Week

I get that this is not an indictment of late risers or people who are most energetic at night; it is instead, a lesson that the amount of work I am willing to do to achieve a thing increases my chances of achieving that thing.

My Action Step

In 2010, when I committed to learn about investing, I immediately began using the four things I knew would help me learn: (1) I met *people* who know about investing; (2) I learned *words* investors use; (3) I made *decisions* to take classes, go to seminars, read books, read magazine articles, open a brokerage account, and learn how to evaluate companies; (4) I took *action* by attending classes, going to seminars, reading books, reading magazine articles, opening a brokerage account, and learning how to evaluate companies to invest in.

Date:

Your thought for the week: What is one example of how you are "rising early" to make yourself a better manager of your money?

Your action step:

Week 21

"It's not that I'm so smart, it's just that I stay with problems longer."

—Albert Einstein

My Thought for the Week

At one of my graduations, my brother, the late Robert B. Ingram, PhD, gave me a card. In the card, he wrote the importance of perseverance for success in life. He went on to write that talent, intellect, and even luck, were less important than a white-hot commitment to stick to a task until it is done.

My Action Step

Good habits and bad ones are built through stubbornness or perseverance and repetition. I used to smoke cigarettes when I was younger. The first time I puffed on one, its taste was bitter, my eyes watered, and I coughed. A year later, I was smoking a pack a day. My stubbornness overcame resistance, and I developed a habit. When I decided to quit, my body had become so used to smoking that it took perseverance to break the habit; neither knowledge, talent, nor luck alone or together could do it. Perseverance and faith broke the habit. What do cigarettes have to do with money management? Without rattling off a bunch of numbers, you will probably forget, aside from the cost of the cigarettes, the added medical costs, and increased insurance premiums are staggering over the course of your life.

Date:

Your thought for the week: Name one area of your life where persistence has benefitted you financially.

Your action step:

Week 22

"If the first plan you adopt does not work successfully, replace it with a new plan. If this new plan fails to work, replace it, in turn, with still another, and so on until you find a plan which does work."

—Napoleon Hill, *Think and Grow Rich*

My Thought for the Week

There is a difference between stubbornness and perseverance. When you want to achieve something, stubbornness is blindly sticking to your plan even when it is not working. Perseverance is adjusting and refining your plan until you achieve what you set out to do.

My Action Step

As a good money manager, I am willing to adjust my plan as new information becomes available. I transferred some money from a credit union to a bank because the credit union's service and policies were inferior to the bank's service and policies.

Date:

Your thought for the week: In what way have you adjusted a plan for your money because the other way was not working?

Your action step:

Week 23

"An ounce of action is worth a ton of theory."

—Fredrich Engels

My Thought for the Week

I have exercised (lifted weights, jogged, cycled, swam) since I was a teenager. One thing I learned early on is that, any exercise is better than no exercise. One of my friends has weighed around 280 pounds and constantly talked about beginning elaborate exercise programs. I tried to explain to him that walking twenty minutes a day will get you better results than thinking about running twenty miles a day, but he never got the lesson.

My Action Step

For a couple of years, I had a mock account with $1 million in fake money. I bought and sold stocks fearlessly, making and losing money. I had brilliant ideas about why one company was better than the other. I opened an actual investment account with $100 real dollars in it. I was amazed at how afraid I was to lose the real $100 when losing $10,000 in fake money didn't bother me at all. That was the difference between the theory of losing $10,000 versus the reality of losing $100.

Date:

Your thought for the week: What ounce of action will you take today with your money?

Your action step:

Week 24

"The best time to plant a tree was twenty years ago. The second-best time is now."

—Chinese Proverb

My Thought for the Week

One thing I must be on guard against when I learn something new and valuable is regretting that I did not learn it sooner. It took as long as it took for me to learn it and what is most important is what I do after I learn it.

My Action Step

When I first started working, I immediately had money deducted from my paycheck to go into savings. The job also offered deferred compensation that would have allowed me to contribute pretax dollars to a fund that could grow in a tax-deferred account until I retired and was ready to withdraw it. I was on the job for more than ten years before I took advantage of it. When I did, I immediately calculated how much I would have had if I had started ten years sooner—a lot. It was what it was. I could not get back those ten years; all I could do was the best I could going forward.

Date:

Your thought for the week: What seeds are you planting in your money garden today?

Your action step:

Week 25

"An investment in knowledge pays the best interest."

—Benjamin Franklin

My Thought for the Week

Once you have developed the habit of giving and saving money from all that you get, you must be about the business of accumulating knowledge about the money you get, give, and save.

My Action Step

The water bill at my brother's house averaged thirty dollars a month, which was billed quarterly. One quarter, the bill was $600. We learned that the toilet in the guest bathroom was leaking, and in ninety days, it caused his bill to jump 2,000 percent. In 2004, I began devoting ten or fifteen minutes a week to learning good money habits. Just as that leak caused the bill to jump, the slow accumulation of knowledge caused my ability to manage money to grow and expand enormously.

Date:

Your thought for the week: What ways are you growing your knowledge about your money?

Your action step:

Week 26

"Everybody can't be quarterback."

—Dr. Thomas Kenneth Pinder
A police officer who mentored me when I was a kid

My Thought for the Week

What he meant by this was; you don't have to play every position on the team to win. I don't have to know everything about money to be a good money manager. I can put a team in place that knows and does the things I am not good at or do not choose to do.

My Action Step

I was once audited by the Internal Revenue Service and had to pay a hefty sum. Ironically, I did not do my own taxes, but paid someone to do them for me. From that, I learned never to use that person again, as well as how to keep better records and prepare my own tax returns. When my wife and I started our first company, we hired a certified public accountant to do our taxes. I concerned myself with my position of running the business, while I let my CPA handle the position of preparing the business tax returns. We hired a lawyer to fill the position of incorporating us. We utilized other professionals and contractors on a project-by-project basis. Everybody can't be quarterback, but if each of us plays our respective positions, we can still win.

Date:

Your thought for the week: What position do you want to play on your money-making team, and what positions do you want others to play?

Your action step:

Week 27

"The best way, the best chance you've got of improving your situation, is to think differently from what you've been thinking in the past and think differently from how most other people think."

—Dolf de Roos, PhD, *How to Take Your Business Global*

My Thought for the Week

I started life poor (youngest of eleven children, terminally ill father, and mother on welfare). I knew at a young age, that for that to change in my life time, I had to think differently from some of the ways I was being taught and from the ways many of the people around me thought.

My Action Step

One of my greatest blessings in life was, is, and will continue to be my passion for reading. Through reading, I have been able to constantly infuse new and better ideas into my thinking about God, life, love, money, and many other things.

Date:

Your thought for the week: In what ways can you begin to think differently from how you and others around you have been thinking about money?

Your action step:

Week 28

"Every professional executes with the anticipation of success. The professional golfer expects to hole the putt, the quarterback expects to complete the pass, and every baseball player comes to bat expecting to get a hit."
—Harvey Reese, *How to License your Million Dollar Idea*

My Thought for the Week

I look forward to a lifetime of accumulating money that will make me more money and to giving money to people, groups, organizations, or causes I am on fire for.

My Action Step

I have savings and giving accounts, where I deposit money so that when I receive money, it immediately goes into each of those accounts before I pay for anything else. When it is time to invest or to give, the money has already been set aside.

Date:

Your thought for the week: What type of financial success are you anticipating in your future?

Your action step:

Week 29

"You have powers you never dreamed of. You can do things you never thought you could do. There are no limitations in what you can do except in your own mind."

Darwin P. Kingsley, President, New York Life

My Thought for the Week

The movies I allow to play in the theater of my mind will project themselves into the reality of my life. By first seeing myself doing things I have never done before and then doing them, I will continually expand the possibilities of my life.

My Action Step

I was in college when I bought my first brand-new car—a maroon hatchback Datsun 310GX with no air conditioning (in Florida, where the temperatures get into the nineties). With my part-time job, I made just enough to cover the payments, insurance, and gas. Until then, I had driven a string of jalopies, some of which only lasted a couple of months before I sold them to the junkyard for scrap metal. Once I exceeded the old limit of buying used clunkers, buying new cars became easy. I can't even remember how many new cars I have had so far.

Date:

Your thought for the week: In your mind's eye, what thing do you see yourself doing with money that you have never done before?

Your action step:

Week 30

"I have learned that only through focus can you do great things, no matter how capable you are."

—William H. Gates, Microsoft founder

My Thought for the Week

The *Merriam-Webster* dictionary defines focus as, "a center of activity, attraction, or attention." Experience has taught me when I have wanted something badly in my life, that by centering my activities and attention on the thing, either I was attracted to it or it was attracted to me.

My Action Step

I used to keep a poster with a picture of Paris, France on my wall, because it was one of my dream destinations. I wanted to drink coffee while sitting at a sidewalk café on the Champs-Élysées. In 1995, my best friend, Irving Thomas, was playing professional basketball in France. For my birthday, he flew me over for an all-expenses-paid vacation to include drinking coffee while sitting at a sidewalk café on Champs-Élysées. Thanks, Irv.

Date:

Your thought for the week: How much money do you want and for what? Do you want it badly enough to center your activity and focus on it until you are attracted to it or it is attracted to you?

Your action step:

Week 31

"The heights by great men reached and kept,
Were not attained by sudden flight
But they while their companions slept
Were toiling upward in the night."

—Henry Wadsworth Longfellow

My Thought for the Week

When I bought the house we now live in, the oak tree along the driveway was about six feet tall, a couple of inches shorter than I am. Although I could not see it growing in real time, all day every day, it grew, until it became more than twice my height. It did not grow suddenly, but continuously.

My Action Step

Like the oak tree, I grow my money and my knowledge about money every day. Like the oak tree outgrew me, my money will outgrow the amount I need to live comfortably all the days of my life.

Date:

Your thought for the week: How are you growing your money so that it outgrows the amount you need to live comfortably for the rest of your life?

Your action step:

Week 32

"I must create a system or be enslaved by another man's."

—William Blake

My Thought for the Week

I had a large bottle with a small neck that I wanted to capture rain water in. I could use a funnel with a wide cone and a narrow spout. By putting the narrow spout in the bottleneck, the wide cone could collect water then and funnel it into the bottle. If I allow someone else to place their cone above mine, that person could not divert the rain water to his or her bottle causing my bottle to stay empty.

My Action Step

When I was around five years old, my mom bought me a small combination safe with a slot to drop coins into. Once I set the combination, only I could open it. Whenever I got coins (back then, a quarter could buy something), I would put them in the safe. That safe was a funnel that caused the coins coming into my life to go into and stay in my bottle, before someone else, like the ice cream man or the corner store clerk or one of my sticky-fingered cousins could funnel them into their pockets.

Date:

Your thought for the week: How are you funneling money into your bottles before it goes into the bottles of others?

Your action step:

Week 33

"Panic is not a strategy."

—Liz Ann Sonders, Charles Schwab & Co.

My Thought for the Week

I understand that accidents happen. People get sick, valuables get stolen, money gets lost. Such are the inevitable ups and downs of life. I do not know when, where, how or which one will be my challenge; therefore, rather than panic when it happens, I will create a plan to protect me whenever something adverse does happen.

My Action Step

I became a big believer in insurance at a young age. When I was a teenager, my sister who was a few years older than I, got married, had a new child, and decided to buy a used car. To save money, she held off on insuring the car, figuring she would buy the insurance with her next paycheck. Her husband got into an accident and totaled the car before it was insured. If memory serves, the loan amount was over $9,000, which my sister—honest as the sun is bright—continued to pay even though the car could not be fixed. I have had twelve new cars in my life and never gone a single day without insurance. I understand accidents happen, and I choose to be prepared instead of preparing to panic.

Date:

Your thought for the week: What types of insurance do you need or have?

Your action step:

Week 34

"I hate to be wrong. That has aborted many a tempting error but not all of them. But I hate much more to stay wrong."

—Paul A. Samuelson, American Economist

My Thought for the Week

I once watched a politician being interviewed on television. A reporter was criticizing the politician for changing his mind on an issue. The politician told the reporter, "That's what I do when I make a mistake. What do you do?"

My Action Step

The last time I bought a van, I went to a different dealer who not only leased me the van but let me have it for no money down and lowered my payment one hundred dollars a month. I happened to run into the guy who sold me my previous van, and he told me he could have beat that deal. My obvious question was, *if three years ago you could have given me a better deal, why didn't you?* I hated being wrong, but I would have hated staying wrong by letting him sell me another van.

Date:

Your thought for the week: What one mistake about your money do you need to make right?

Your action step:

Week 35

"Every morning in Africa a gazelle wakes up. It knows it must run faster than the fastest lion or it will be killed. Every morning a lion wakes up. It knows it must run faster than the slowest gazelle or it will starve to death. It doesn't matter whether you are a lion or a gazelle, when the sun comes up, you better start running."

—African Proverb

My Thought for the Week

In my lifelong quest to be a good money manager, at times, I will be paid money for goods and services I provide and at other times, I will pay money for goods and services provided to me. It does not matter which one I am doing now; what matters is that whoever pays me, gets my best and whomever I pay, gives me their best.

My Action Step

When I was ready to buy another car, a friend of mine wanted to buy my 310GX, which by then was three years old and paid for. Because I cared for my friend, I put an air conditioner in the car, painted the rims, and had a complete mechanical check done on the car before I would let the friend buy it. My friend paid me a fair price for the best deal I could offer, and I offered the dealer a fair price for the best car he could supply.

Date:

Your thought for the week: When it comes to getting money, how are you giving your best? When it comes to paying someone, how are you sure you are getting their best?

Your action step:

Week 36

"Strategy and smarts beat capital nine times out of ten."

—John W. Henry

My Thought for the Week

I know of two people in my life who inherited what I consider large amounts of money. One received over $25,000 from an insurance policy and the other a three-bedroom, two-bathroom house that was paid for. Within five years, the one who got the house lost it due to nonpayment of taxes. The one who got the money lasted a little longer, but after ten years was flat broke and twenty years later, still broke.

My Action Step

If you cannot manage small things well, it is unlikely you will manage the larger things any better. Retired NBA player James Jones said he cut yards when he was a kid, and his mother forced him to save some of what he made until he developed the habit for himself. Because he knew how to manage a little money, when he got his NBA contract, managing a lot of money came easy to him. By learning how to pay my bills on time when I was working part-time, I could continue paying them since I have been making good money.

Date:

Your thought for the week: What is your strategy for the money you get?

Your action step:

Week 37

"Even being right three or four times out of ten should yield a person a fortune if he has the sense to cut his losses quickly on the ventures where he has been wrong."

—Bernard Baruch (Financier, speculator, statesman, presidential adviser, 1870–1965)

My Thought for the Week

This is one of the most difficult concepts because it runs contrary to the tenet of persistence. So, it can be best illustrated with what a car's GPS (global positioning system) does. Once you put in your destination, if you veer from the suggested route, the GPS redirects you back toward your destination. The key here is knowing your destination first. In doing this, you can objectively assess if the route you are taking is getting you closer or further from it.

My Action Step

My goals are that whenever I get money, to increase the amount I have given away by giving more away and to increase the amount I have kept by saving some of it. If each time I get money, I don't put some into a short-term savings account, some into a long-term savings account, and some towards a charity, I must adjust my plan until that becomes automatic and understood.

Date:

Your thought for the week: Where is your money destination, and what turns do you need to make to ensure you get there?

Your action step:

Week 38

"Before everything else, getting ready is the secret to success."

—Henry Ford

My Thought for the Week

My brother, Ronald, told me a long time ago that everybody wants to win, but not everybody is willing to do what it takes to win. When my sons were younger, they both played "rec" basketball. I taught them that the better prepared you are for practice, the better you practice, and the better you practice, the better you are prepared to play.

My Action Step

Preparing a plan for handling my money better prepares me for what to do with the money as it comes.

Date:

Your thought for the week: Describe an important part of your money plan.

Your action step:

Week 39

"I have not failed. I've just found ten thousand ways that won't work...Many of life's failures are people who did not realize how close they were to success when they gave up."

—Thomas Alba Edison

My Thought for the Week

Inside every mistake is a learning opportunity. As I learn about managing my money, I will inevitably make some mistakes. I may loan money to someone who does not pay it back, invest in a stock that tanks, buy a car that is a lemon, and on and on. Whatever the mistake, I will review what happened carefully, take ownership of what I did, and then press forward with the new knowledge I acquired.

My Action Step

The first notebook computer I bought, for $1,100, was a dud. The screen was not bright enough, the keyboard's keys were not smooth, and the programs were not what I needed. When I went to return it, the company charged me a 10 percent restocking fee. From that, I learned: (1) read the refund policy carefully, (2) look at at least three similar products before deciding to buy a big-ticket item, and (3) whenever possible, wait twenty-four hours before you buy the item. If you sleep on it, chances are that the next day, you will realize there was something you forgot to ask. These rules have saved me money time after time.

Date:

Your thought for the week: What ways of handling your money do not work and need to be changed to ways that do?

Your action step:

Week 40

"No investigation, no right to speak."

—Confucius

My Thought for the Week

When it came to money, I would often hear people parrot the opinions of others, as though the opinions were facts, even though the speaker never verified them. One I still hear today is, "Remember, when you retire, you will be making less money than when you were working." That is not true for everybody. What many of these well-intentioned people were doing was repeating things as facts although they never verified whether they were true.

My Action Step

Whenever I used to talk to people about investing in the stock market, most of them said with conviction that they were scared and warned me not to do it because I would lose money. Once I began studying for myself, I would ask them, "How many stocks have you bought?" The answer was usually none, but I heard…They had reached their conclusions without ever investigating their ideas to see if they were valid or not. When I decided to invest in the stock market, I read books, read articles, joined a club, spoke with brokers, invested in a mock portfolio, and eventually, bought my first stock. Win or lose, I planned to act based on my own investigations rather than on the untested opinions of others.

Date:

Your thought for the week: What opinions about money are you parroting rather than investigating?

Your action step:

Week 41

"Poverty is attracted to the mind of the one who is favorable to it, as money is attracted to one whose mind has been deliberately prepared to attract it, and through the same laws."

—Napoleon Hill *Think and Grow Rich*

My Thought for the Week

There is a Cherokee legend in which a grandfather tells his grandson the good wolf (joy, peace, love…) and the bad wolf (anger, envy, sorrow…). The grandfather explains the two wolves are fighting inside him. When the grandson asks which wolf will win, the grandfather answers, "The one you feed."

My Action Step

Growing up on welfare, I dreaded the idea that I might stay poor all my life. I also dreamed that I could work hard and create a better life for myself. I fed the dream, and the dream continues to win.

Date:

Your thought for the week: Which ideas about money are you feeding?

Your action step:

Week 42

"Many a false step was made by standing still."

--FORTUNE COOKIE

My Thought for the Week

I will not let a fear of making a mistake keep me from making a move toward the things I desire.

My Action Step

Every decision I make about money will not be correct, but inside every incorrect decision is an opportunity to learn and get better, which is what I will do.

Date:

Your thought for the week: What type of financial success are you anticipating in your future?

Your action step:

Week 43

"Nobody cares more about your money than you."

—Mike Richter, my first financial advisor

My Thought for the Week

When using a financial advisor, I will remember that in boxing, the coach is not the one throwing punches or getting knocked out; the fighter must still train, execute, and adjust. It is the advisor's job to advise, but that does not relieve me of my responsibility to verify and cross-check the advice, because it is my money, and I am the one who stands to lose the most in a bad decision.

My Action Step

A friend of mine was having some financial challenges and asked my wife and me to loan him some money to help get his business started. He said he would sign whatever note I wanted, pay whatever interest I asked for, and put up whatever collateral was needed for me to know my money was secured. We loaned him the money with no note, no collateral, and no interest, because in our minds, his character was surety for the return of our money. Within six months, he paid us back with 10 percent interest and took me, my wife, and kids to a Sunday brunch on Fort Lauderdale Beach to say thank you.

Date:

Your though for the week: In what ways do you care more about your money than the person advising you?

Your action step:

Week 44

"If you fail to plan, you are planning to fail."

—Benjamin Franklin

My Thought for the Week

For argument's sake, let's say I am in Miami, Florida, and want to go to Atlanta, Georgia. If I took a shiny white Bentley Flying Spur, filled it with gas, pointed it due south, and drove as fast as legally possible, I would not make it to Atlanta, because it is north of Miami. Having no direction for your money to go in is like driving fast with no plan for where you want to end up.

My Action Step

In 2004, I seriously began my plan to be a good money manager for the rest of my life. I committed to taking notes and learning one new thing a week about money.

Date:

Your thought for the week: What is your plan for managing your money?

Your action step:

Week 45

"Never argue with a pig. It just frustrates you and irritates the pig."

—Unknown

My Thought for the Week

When people say things like, "I am so broke, I can't pay attention" or "I am going to die in debt" or "It was your fault for loaning me the money, which you knew I wouldn't pay you back," I will not argue with them, but I will make it my business to have no money dealings with them.

My Action Step

Because I care about people, when I hear them speak defeat over their lives, I will gently suggest that they can change. If, however, they are not open to the possibility of change, I will not argue to convince them, because it will most likely frustrate me and irritate them.

Date:

Your thought for the week: What self-defeating words about money do I need to root out of my speaking and thinking?

Your action step:

Week 46

"Good luck is what happens when preparation meets opportunity. Bad luck is what happens when lack of preparation meets a challenge."

—Paul Krugman (Economist, NY Times)

My Thought for the Week

There was a short-lived reality television show that followed people who won the lottery for millions of dollars. I was amazed at the number of winners who were broke within a couple of years. The winners who did keep their money were people who had good money management skills before they were ever lucky enough to win.

My Action Step

I have friends, professional associates (lawyers, doctors, accountants), and friends who not only know how to work for money but know how to get money to work for them.

Date:

Your thought for the week: How are you preparing for your good luck when it comes?

Your action step:

Week 47

"As a blind comedian once said, when you're blind and lazy, people think you're just blind."

—Isaac Lidsky, *Eyes Wide Open*

My Thought for the Week

I am not perfect, so I am vulnerable to blind spots in how I see things. I accept that, and I am not afraid to partner with people who can see what I may not.

My Action Step

Once at work, I was furious at one of my supervisors for something I was sure he did, and I let him know how I felt, even though he said he did not do what I thought he did. Later, my friend, Joe, told me he had overheard the entire thing, and the supervisor had nothing to do with what happened. It was one of my coworkers that I never suspected. Thankfully, Joe saw what I could not. Rather than be blind and lazy, I apologized for my error.

Date:

Your thought for the week: What money area might you be blind in and need someone else to help you see better?

Your action step:

Week 48

"Optimism means expecting the best, but confidence means knowing how to handle the worst. Never make a move if you are merely optimistic."

–Unknown

My Thought for the Week

Although I expect success when I attempt something new or different, I know some things I do will not turn out as I expect. Therefore, I never try something new or different without knowing the risk of how much I could lose if it does not go as expected.

My Action Step

I buy and read books because the downside risk is the cost of the book, but the potential gain of learning something new that I can use is unlimited. One of the key axioms of successful investing is limited downside risk versus unlimited upside gain.

Date:

Your thought for the week: What is the downside risk and upside potential of at least one thing you are doing with your money?

Your action step:

Week 49

"No matter what you want out of life, four things will help you or hinder you from getting those things: *(1) the people you know*, (2) the words you know, (3) the decisions you make, and (4) the actions you take."

—Laurick Ingram

My Thought for the Week

There is a real estate investor who opened one of his presentations with a question. "Who in the audience wants to have ten million dollars?" Inevitably, nearly every hand went up. He followed up with the question, "How many people do you personally know that have ten million dollars?" Inevitably, only a few, if any, hands went up. The obvious takeaway is that you have a group of people who want to get something in life, but they do not associate with people who have gotten that thing and could teach others how to do it.

My Action Step

When I wanted to learn how to box, I found a boxing coach, a boxing gym, and worked out with other boxers. I never got to compete—that was not my goal—but I ended up in much better shape, knowing a lot more about boxing than before I met those people. When I wanted to get better at handling money, I hired a CPA, joined an investment club, and looked for and learned from people who handled money better than I did.

Date:

Your thought for the week: Who are the people you know or should know that can help you in your fight to get, give, and save your money?

Your action step:

Week 50

"No matter what you want out of life, four things will help you or hinder you from getting those things: (1) the people you know, *(2) the words you know* (3) the decisions you make, and (4) the actions you take."

—Laurick Ingram

My Thought for the Week

Whatever my chosen field of endeavor, the better handle I have on the words used by those in that field, the better I will understand what is going on. If my banker is offering to sell me a CD, chances are she means certificate of deposit not compact disc. Words matter.

My Action Step

When discussing money matters, I have a working knowledge of terms like return on investment, interest rate, common stock, debt to income ratio, and the like. Those words are assets to me that add value to my ability to evaluate good versus bad money decisions.

Date:

Your thought for the week: What words do you know and are you learning to help you master your money?

Your action step:

Week 51

"No matter what you want out of life, four things will help you or hinder you from getting those things: (1) the people you know, (2) the words you know (3) *the decisions you make*, and (4) the actions you take.

—Laurick Ingram

My Thought for the Week

Cat: "Where are you going?"
Alice: "Which way should I go?"
Cat: "That depends on where you are going."
Alice: "I don't know."
Cat: "Then it doesn't matter which way you go."

—Lewis Carroll, *Alice in Wonderland*

My Action Step

I had to decide a long time ago what money road I would take. The one that led to a life of believing that money constantly flows out of my life and that I will never have enough money, or the one that led to a life of believing that money constantly flows into my life. I will always have more money than I need. I decided to take the latter road, and it makes all the difference.

Date:

Your thought for the week: What money road will you decide to take?

Your action step:

Week 52

"No matter what you want out of life, four things will help you or hinder you from getting those things: (1) the people you know, (2) the words you know (3) the decisions you make, and *(4) the actions you take.*"

—Laurick Ingram

My Thought for the Week

I close with the parable of the ten birds. If ten birds are sitting on a fence, and one decides to fly away, how many birds are left on the fence? Ten birds are left, because deciding to fly is not the same as flapping your wings and taking off.

My Action Step

Right here, right now, I will continually grow my money management skills by applying the things I have learned in this book.

Date:

Your thought for the week: What action do you plan to take with your money?

Your action step:

AFTERWORD

Give and Save 365, LLC, was founded by my wife and me. The Give and Save 3-6-5 core concept is creating prosperity through philanthropy. We believe in growing your giving through faith and growing your faith through saving. Our mission is, "Teaching you how to use every dollar you get to add value to your life and the lives of others." I agree with Stephen Covey that teaching something requires a deeper understanding than just learning it. I am encouraging you not only to develop your own lifetime habit of giving and saving, but to teach at least one other person what you have learned.

Thank you for sharing your precious time with us.

Be blessed!

Laurick Ingram

ABOUT THE AUTHOR

Laurick, also known as the Give and Save Guy, embodies the Give and Save 3-6-5 Concept of creating prosperity through philanthropy. Each week he recognizes a person or organization doing good in the community and the world. He donates then requests others donate to help these people and organizations continue their good works. For every dollar he gives, he saves an equal amount to better himself and his family. He believes people can grow their giving through faith and grow their faith through saving. The United Nations Association (Broward Chapter) honored him for his efforts to eradicate poverty. He has been interviewed on radio and television and has been mentioned on more than 100 journals and publications.

He lives in South Florida with his wife, Kim, and their two sons, Joshua and Jawanza. Laurick was the youngest of 11 children and grew up in the James E. Scott Housing Projects of Liberty City. He graduated from Miami Central High School (Go Rockets!), then worked his way through Miami-Dade College, earning a degree in Business Administration. He is a long-time member of Polaris Investment Club (West Palm Beach, Florida), which is a Chapter of Better Investing.